COPYRIGHT 2018, 2017 by Pinecrest Street Company

All rights reserved. This publication is protected by Copyright laws. No part of this book may be reproduced, stored in a retrieval system, or transmitted in any form, or by any means electronic, mechanical, photocopying, recording, or otherwise with prior permission of Pinecrest Street Company, and as expressly permitted by the applicable copyright status. Dissemination or sale of any part of this book is not permitted. Request for written permission may be obtained by writing Pinecrest Street Company, LLC. 11301 S. Dixie Hwy. Box 5666684, Miami FL 33256. Pinecrest Street Company crest is a trademark of Pinecrest Street Company, Inc. and is registered in the United States.
ISBN 978-0-9995575-9-4

Executive Editor: Carlos Borges
Authors: Kay Lopate and Patsy Self Trand
Book Design and Layout: Ana Garcia and Alexa Behm
Published independently by Pinecrest Street Company, LLC.
www.pinecreststreetcompany.com
Address 11301 S. Dixie Hwy. Box 566684 Miami FL 33156
Printed in the United States

TAKING ON THE CHALLENGE SERIES

THE OFFICIAL
Parent
PLAYBOOK

GETTING YOUR CHILD THROUGH COLLEGE

EXPERT ADVICE FROM COLLEGE PROFESSORS
RESEARCHED AND WRITTEN BY

KAY LOPATE, PH. D.   PATSY SELF TRAND, PH. D.

Books Published by Pinecrest Street Company, Inc.

College Bound Series: Knowing What to Expect – Preparing for "A's"

30 Awesome reading and learning strategies for high school students. (2017). Trand, Patsy Self and Lopate, Kay. Pinecrest Street Company.

Become a great college reader: Get the basics of reading now before you begin college. Book 1. (2017). Lopate, Kay and Trand, Patsy Self. Pinecrest Street Company.

Getting the basics of critical thinking for college readers and writers. Book 2. (2018). Lopate, Kay and Trand, Patsy Self. Pinecrest Street Company.

Challenge Series: Success in Difficult Courses – Making "A's"

Making it to Graduation: Expert advice from college professors (2nd, ed.) (2018). Lopate, Kay and Trand, Patsy Self. Pinecrest Street Company.

The Official Parent Playbook: Getting your child through college. (2nd, ed.) (2018) Lopate, Kay and Trand, Patsy Self. Pinecrest Street Company.

Making it in Medical School: Expert advice from college professors. (2019). Lopate, Kay and Trand, Patsy Self. Pinecrest Street Company.

Making it in Nursing School: Expert advice from college professors. (2019). Trand, Patsy Self, and Lopate, Kay. Pinecrest Street Company.

The athletes' playbook for college success. (2018). Trand, Patsy Self and Lopate, Kay. Pinecrest Street Company.

"Vocabulary university professors say that every college student should know. (2017). Trand, Patsy Self and Lopate, Kay. Pinecrest Street Company.

Navigating Through College and Beyond Series – Making more "A's"

Capturing the Experience: My child's first year in college. (2nd, ed.) (2017) Lopate, Kay and Trand, Patsy Self, Carpenter, Sara, Pinecrest Street Company.

Capturing the Experience: My first year in college. (2nd, ed.) (2017) Lopate, Kay and Trand, Patsy Self, Carpenter, Sara, Pinecrest Street Company.

Reading and Learning the Required College Courses in the Historical and Social Sciences. Book 3. (2017). Trand, Patsy Self and Lopate, Kay. Pinecrest Street Company.

Reading and Learning the Required College Courses in the Biological and Mathematical Sciences. Book 4 (2017). Trand, Patsy Self and Lopate, Kay. Pinecrest Street Company.

30 Amazing reading and learning strategies for college students. (2017). Lopate, Kay and Trand, Patsy Self. Pinecrest Street Company.

Why I didn't come to class. (2018). Trand, Patsy Self and Lopate, Kay. Pinecrest Street Company.

PINECREST STREET COMPANY, LLC.
Pinecrest Street Publishing
www.pinecreststreetcompany.com
Pinecrest Street Company, LLC
11301 S. Dixie Hwy. POBox 566684
Pinecrest, FL 33256

Table of Contents

1 Introduction

3 Letter to Yourself

6 Summer "To-Do" List
A. Money matters (6)
B. Planners (8)
C. What to "Pick-Up" Before Your Child Goes To College
    1. Learning tools (13)
    2. Dorm room items (14)
    3. Clothes (15)
    4. Contact information (16)

18 Get to Know the University
1. Orientation (18)
2. Orientation List (20)
3. Groups (22)
4. Living on the campus (24)
5. Know the campus/university (26)

28 Using Time Wisely

30 Grade Point Average

32 Warning Signs

36 Helping Your Child Stay Thoughtful and Considerate

40 Dealing With Friends and Peers

42 Keeping a Good Relationship with Your Child

46 Helping Academically

50 Providing Encouragement

54 Extra Caring Gestures

58 Expectations

62 Parents—REMEMBER THESE POINTERS: THE DO'S and DONT'S

68 Appendix

73 Index

76 Final Thoughts

78 Follow-up Letter to Yourself

WELCOME TO COLLEGE!

After months of helping with entrance exams, campus visits, the high school graduation process, and dealing with your child's emotional ups and downs, your child is now a college student. Don't be surprised if your emotions swing from being happy and excited one moment and then feeling sad and worried the next. Remember, you have looked forward to this milestone for a long time. Remind yourself that your job as a parent continues beyond age 18. Keep reassuring yourself that your child knows that you and your family will always be there for support and understanding.

We hope this book helps you and your child make a smooth and successful transition to college. We encourage you to take the time to read this book (cover to cover) before the first day of classes. You may want to review it again during the semester.

On the next page, write a letter to yourself. Notice that each paragraph begins with a sentence starter. All you need to do is add 2-3 sentences to complete the paragraph.

Writing the letter at the beginning of college and then reading it at graduation, may bring many surprises. We hope it makes you happy and creates a lot of good memories for you!

Date: _____

Dear: _____

As I watch my child move on to college, _____
_____
_____

I think what I will miss the most is: _____
_____
_____

I will probably worry about: _____
_____

However, I am really happy because _____
_____

Regards to myself,
_____

"

THE MOST **IMPORTANT** THING THAT A PARENT CAN TEACH THEIR CHILDREN IS HOW TO GET ALONG **WITHOUT THEM.**

—

FRANK A. CLARK

"

Summer TO-DO LIST

MONEY *matters*

CHECKLIST

- [ ] Go over your financial situation with your child.

- [ ] Work together to make a financial budget

- [ ] Discuss limits on spending and establish who pays for what.

- [ ] Have an honest, frank talk about the family's financial position. Itemize all expenditures and then estimate how much a four year college education will cost.

    Include:
    tuition, room and board, books, entertainment, travel, clubs dues, clothes, phone/internet, and incidentals.

- [ ] Stress the importance of paying bills on time.

- [ ] If you want your child to have a bank account, consider using a bank that has a branch in your home town.

- [ ] The next time you get a credit card offer in the mail, review it with your child.

- [ ] If you want your child to have a credit card, apply for one four months before your child leaves for college. Some parents favor debit cards. Be sure to let your child know spending limits.

- [ ] Don't hesitate to discuss credit card spending, ID theft, password protection fraud and "rip-offs".

- [ ] Take care that your child knows how to write a check and how to keep track of the money in the account.

- [ ] Help your child decide which meal plan to buy.

Summer TO-DO LIST planners

1 DATES TO REMEMBER.

Buy a monthly planner and fill in family birthdays, anniversaries, holidays, and other important dates. Remind them of the importance of acknowledging these anniversaries and other events.

2 KNOW WHAT TIME IT IS...

Buy an alarm clock even though your child may say the cell phone is also an alarm clock.

3 BUY A THESAURUS AND A DICTIONARY.

4 BUY A LARGE WHITEBOARD (3X3) AND A SET OF COLORED MARKERS.

5 SPACE SAVER...

Pack lightly. Your child doesn't need as much as he/she thinks.

Dorm rooms are usually small with little storage.

6 BUYING BOOKS.

Try to buy textbooks weeks before the semester begins and encourage your child to browse through them.

Did you hear about the banker who was recently arrested for embezzling $100,000 to pay for his daughter's college education?

As the policeman *(who also had a daughter in college)* was leading him away in handcuffs, he asked the banker:

"WHERE WERE YOU GOING TO GET THE REST OF IT?"

Summer TO-DO LIST

What to "pick-up" BEFORE your child GOES TO COLLEGE

LEARNING TOOLS

- ☐ Pens, pencils, paper, filing folders, note cards, and backpack.

- ☐ Separate notebooks for each class.

- ☐ Course Textbooks (keep the receipt of the textbooks and do not take the shrink wrap off until you attend class and the professor identifies that text as necessary)

- ☐ Laptop and/or Smart Phone, flash drives, duct tape, flashlight, surge protectors, adapters, power strips, and noise cancelling headphones.

DORM ROOM ITEMS

- ☐ A trunk that locks with a key for your child to keep valuables.

- ☐ Quick, non-refrigerated foods (such as soup) that can be warmed in the microwave.

- ☐ Sheets (make sure that you get the size of the bed. Most universities order non-standard size mattresses), pillows, and blankets.

- ☐ Towels

- ☐ Washing detergent

- ☐ Personal grooming items and toiletries

- ☐ Hand vacuum

CLOTHES

- ☐ Shoes, sneakers, and sandals that are comfortable for walking across campus.

- ☐ Shorts, jeans, t-shirts, workout clothes, sweat shirts.

- ☐ Dress clothes.

- ☐ Cover-ups, sweaters, and coats for warm and cold.

- ☐ Weather and rain gear.

- ☐ Socks and underwear.

CONTACTS

Place all of the following numbers and addresses on either your cell phone and your child's phone.

- ☐ Friends, grandparents, relatives, family friends, family physician, dentist, insurance providers.

- ☐ Neighbor's phone number or someone who can physically and quickly get to your parent's home in case of an emergency and your parents cannot be reached by phone.

- ☐ Physician's names and phone number.

- ☐ Phone number of pharmacy in case prescriptions or pharmacy accounts need to be transferred.

- ☐ You and your child need the phone number of campus police and the campus saftey escort.

Additionally, get the phone numbers of non- emergency lines.

"

WHEN I WAS IN COLLEGE I WAS EXPOSED TO A WORLD I DIDN'T KNOW WAS POSSIBLE.

—

TOM HANKS

GET TO KNOW THE University

ORIENTATION

BECOME A PART
Orientation is designed to connect students and parents so they both feel a part of the new environment.

TAKE NOTES
Parents should plan to attend all orientation sessions. Bring lots of questions and take notes.

DO A WALK THROUGH
Become very familiar with the campus, your child's new environment. Before the first day of classes, do a "walk through" of your child's schedule. This will give you a better idea of situations when you talk to your child.

TAKE NAMES
Get the names of presenters at orientation sessions. They are usually the "key" people.

MEET THE PARENTS
Meet other parents. In most cases you will be seeing them again.

FAMILIARIZE
Learn about all the campus resources.

EASE THE ANXIETY
Orientation helps reduce the anxiety and separation fear that parents and students face.

ONJOUR HOLA HELLO GUTEN TAG
LÀ CIAO NAMASTE مرحبا JAMBO
ABARI CAU AWEH こんにち
は HALO 你好 G'DAY N'TATE
UDAVINUN HALLO HEJ MESIERE
IA DHUIT RAZ CZESC
AMUSTA
ALAM ALL ERHABA JURU
U VAMB VOUS YASSO
여보세 HOLA HELLO
UTEN TA AO NAMASTE
JAMBO ARI CAU AWEH
مرحبا
こんにちは HALO 你好
DAY N'TATE GUDAVINUN HALLO
EJ MESIERE DIA DHUIT
AOOBRAZ CZESC KAMUSTA
مرحبا BONJOUR HOLA HELLO GUTEN
hello!

GET TO KNOW THE University

ORIENTATION LIST

THE LIBRARY
Visit the library and locate study areas. Also, introduce yourselves to the resource librarian.

"HELP!"
Learn how to contact campus police.

SUPPORT
Your child is not the only one going through a transitional time—most parents are also going through an emotional and stressful time. It is helpful if you can meet these other parents at orientation.

TRANSPORTATION
Learn to navigate the public transportation system.

STUDY AREAS
Find study areas. You might have to be creative and find little "nooks" that can facilitate study even though it is not designed for as a study area. During the parent orientation sessions, ask about study areas that are designated and areas that can double as study areas.

DOCUMENTS
Help your child get a parking decal, student ID, and bicycle permit.

EMOTIONS
Manage your emotions. Resist the temptation to tell your child how sad you will be feeling when it's time to leave.

SAYING GOODBYE

**Before you leave the campus,
you might want to say something like this:**

"We love you just the way you are but now you will have a chance to redefine and recreate yourself while in college."

It's OK to say, **'I'll miss you'** but make sure your child you will be fine. Never say, **'What will I do without you?'**

Don't let your younger children see you upset (and weepy) because the older one has left for college.

Remind yourself that you spent eighteen years building your child's foundation.

You will never completely **"let go"** — you will always be connected in many ways.

HEALTHY SCHEDULE

Many students try to fit most of their classes on a Tuesday and Thursday or a Monday, Wednesday, and Friday. This type of schedule promotes too much relaxing and sleeping on the in-between days.

TYPICAL SCHEDULE	DAY	M	T	W	TR	F
	DURATION	50	75	50	75	50

Recommend this schedule to your child. Your child will thank you for your advice, especially during exam time. Taking five exams on 1 – 2 days is tough. Students cannot get excused from exams, like in high school, if there are too many exams on the same day. The adviser will only say, **"well, you made the schedule."**

GET TO KNOW THE University

GROUPS

Tell your child that a real, balanced education exists beyond the classroom.

SUGGEST SOME OF THESE ADDITIONAL GROUPS TO JOIN:

- ☐ Greek Life
- ☐ LGBT
- ☐ Media Volunteer Services
- ☐ Recreational and Intramural Sports
- ☐ Religious Centers
- ☐ Pre-Medical and Pre-Health Organizations
- ☐ Study Abroad
- ☐ Reserve Officers' Training Corps (ROTC) Campus Activities
- ☐ Boards Homecoming Committee
- ☐ Theatre Committee Groups
- ☐ Music Committee Groups
- ☐ Art Committee Groups

GET TO KNOW THE University

LIVING ON CAMPUS

SO LONG!
Remind your child that if the living arrangements are not working out, it's time to start making plans to move.

RADIATE POSITIVITY
Tell your child to select friends who will impact them in a positive way—those who will not drag them down.

H2O COUNTS
Impress upon your child the importance of drinking water to stay properly hydrated.

TAKE CARE
Help your child understand the importance of staying healthy while living in the dorm.

MEET THE R.A.
Be sure to get the phone numbers of the dormitory, and the name and phone number of your child's Resident Assistant (also known as the R.A.).

BE CAUTIOUS
Remind your student to lock doors and safeguard valuables even though they say they trust everyone on the floor.

HIT THE FIELD
Encourage your child to attend some of the football games and a few other sporting events.

BEAUTY REST
Stress the importance of getting 7-8 hours of sleep every night because illness can result from sleep deprivation and "all-nighters".

> *IN ANY GIVEN MOMENT WE HAVE TWO OPTIONS:*
>
> **TO STEP FORWARD INTO GROWTH**
>
> — OR —
>
> **TO STEP BACK INTO SAFETY.**
>
> — ABRAHAM MASLOW

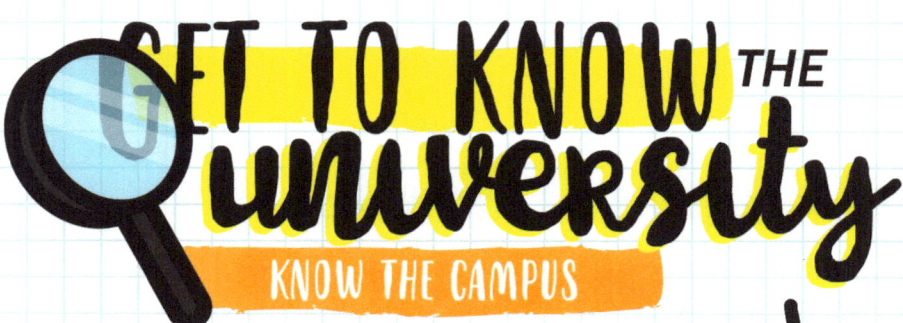

GET TO KNOW THE university

KNOW THE CAMPUS

GREEK LIFE

Discuss the pros and cons of joining a sorority or fraternity. Let them know you need to be a part of this discussion. Ask them if the people in the sorority or fraternity are the ones they want to socialize with for the next four years.

BE INFORMED

Understand the University's Grade Notification Policy and discuss with your child whether or not you will get a copy of the grades.

GET DIRECTION

Make sure you and your child have a campus resource directory for support services.

SEEK ADVICE

Tell your child that students who seek academic advising during a semester have higher graduation rates than those who do not.

BE ONLINE

Stay informed with school events by logging in to the school's website.

HARD WORK PAYS OFF

Let your child know that education is not entertainment and most of the time their classes will not be fun and exciting. A college degree is the result of hard work. Books and lectures are there to convey information and not to entertain.

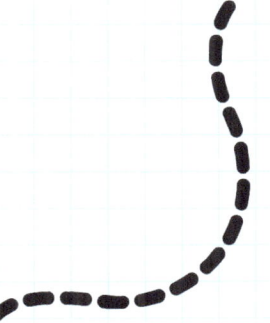

USE TIME WISELY

Discuss the harmful effects of spending too much time online and spending too much time streaming movies and TV series.

If your child must take a nap, tell them **NOT TO NAP** for over an hour.

Encourage your child to set his/her watch **FIVE MINUTES** fast.

Your child has the responsibility to know how much time it takes to learn material for a test. The timing **WILL NOT** be the same as high school.

Remind your child that the biggest **"TIME WASTERS"** are texting, spending time on social media, watching TV, and playing video games.

Encourage your child to be punctual for all appointments, and especially to get to every class on time.

Usually, important announcements are made at the beginning of class. It's disruptive to the instructor and other students when students walk in late.

Demonstrate **"PARKINSON'S LAW"**— Work expands to fill the amount of time allotted to it. Before beginning a task, estimate how long the task should take.

FOR EXAMPLE:
Raking the front yard. Estimate it should take an hour. Chances are if you did not set this time goal, you might still be raking the yard two hours later. Therefore, determine how much time it will take to do every task.

Grade Point Average

Your child will be required to maintain a certain grade point average **(GPA)**. The **GPA** covers two different domains: **semester and cumulative GPA**. The semester **GPA** gives the overall grade average on every term your student is enrolled. The cumulative **GPA** gives the grade point average for the entire time the child was in college. Semester and cumulative **GPA** does not include transfer credits or credits not earned at the specific college/university or which the child will graduate.

All courses taken at colleges and universities other than the institution the child will graduate from **MUST** have ***written approval*** from the advising office. This will ensure that the child's college will accept the course as requirement

fulfilled even though they will not enter the grade into the semester and cumulative **GPA**. Some schools understand the life changes that occur for a student during the transition to college can affect the attention and discipline needed to pass a course. Many schools have a do-over option called **"Grade Forgiveness"** which allows them to retake the failed course. Students must fill out an application to invoke **Grade Forgiveness**. After they have re-taken the failed class, the new passing grade will be applied to their **GPA** instead of the old failing grade.

Please note that ***not all*** colleges offer **Grade Forgiveness**.

BE PREPARED

and don't be alarmed if you get a message saying things are not going well. Just listening to your child's voice on the phone can tell you a lot about how they are doing.
If your child should call with a problem, resist the temptation to rush in immediately.

EXPRESS SUPPORT

but give your child time to solve the problem. You might ask them questions that would lead them to think of possible solutions on their own such as, "What do you think you should do?" This would develop their problem-solving skill and allow them to feel a sense of the autonomy that teenagers crave.

BE CONCERNED

if your child is overly negative about everything.

Look for **"RED FLAGS,"** negative remarks, such as **"I don't like my classes," "the professor is unfair,"** or **"I hate my roommate."** These are warning signs and you may need to follow up with your child's advisor and/or the health center.

Keep advice to a minimum unless they ask for advice. If they ask for advice, use gentle words--- suggest rather than demand.

Sometimes you can tell a lot about your child's emotional state by listening to them. If you feel a face-to-face meeting with your child is the next step, arrange for a time and place to meet.

When you get a phone call asking for help, say **"I think you can handle this"** more often than "OK, I'll take care of this." Be prepared for a "meltdown" phone call. Let your child vent but listen patiently and show concern but suggest to "sleep on it" for a few days. Many young people only call when they are "down". It's a good idea to tell them **NOT EVERY DAY IS GOING TO BE GREAT.**

Find out if your child is not going to class.

Your child may hesitate to tell you about some challenges he/she is facing. **Assure them you will listen without judgement.** Keep in mind your child does not want to disappoint you. Whatever you do, don't scold or tell them what to do. Instead, offer options and possible resources and ask what course of action they might consider.

SUGGEST an impartial listener such as a counselor from the University Guidance Center.

> I HAVE NO SPECIAL **TALENTS.**
>
> I AM ONLY *passionately* **CURIOUS.**
>
> — **ALBERT EINSTEIN**

WAYS TO HELP YOUR CHILD STAY THOUGHTFUL + CARING

THERE IS MORE TO COLLEGE THAN GETTING AN EDUCATION!

TELL YOUR CHILD

it's ok to make mistakes. Because making mistakes are part of the learning process. In fact, learning is constantly making and correcting mistakes. Hopefully, you will learn from the mistakes!

REMEMBER

faculty members are the ones who have the Power of the grade.

ONCE IN A WHILE

say, *"I love the way you're becoming smarter...your mind is expanding with all this new knowledge."*

BUILD

lifetime relationships in college. **VALUE YOUR FRIENDS.**

ALWAYS

treat custodians and secretaries **WITH RESPECT.**

STRESS

that your child should be polite with faculty members.

ENCOURAGE

your child to be enthusiastic for the achievement of others

KNOW THAT

characteristics such as
- *GENEROSITY*
- *POLITENESS*
- *HONESTY*
- *INTEGRITY*
- *CONFIDENCE*
- *EMPATHY*
- *RESPECT*

do not happen by chance.

REMIND YOUR CHILD...

To show appreciation and gratitude to people who have been helpful, caring, and thoughtful. Just remind them that using the words thank you show that you are an appreciative person.

That their social and personal traits will help them throughout the rest of their lives.

It's very important to write thank you notes. Emailing is OK, but snail mail is better!

To always show respect and behave well in class even if you are the only one.

YOU DIDN'T HAVE A CHOICE ABOUT THE PARENTS YOU INHERITED,

BUT YOU DO HAVE A CHOICE ABOUT THE KIND OF PARENT YOU WILL BE.

MARION WRIGHT EDELMAN

dealing with FRIENDS AND PEERS

MAKE THE BEST — Remember that the cure for *homesickness* is not found at home. It's found in your child making new friends and adapting to the new environment.

NO, THANK YOU! — Remind your child that he or she has the right to say *"no"* when faced with temptations.

WORTH THE WAIT — Tell your child that it may take time to make true friends and that the friends they make during the first few weeks of school may not be the friends they want for the next four years.

THREE STRIKES

Propose that your child give people a second chance... **but not a third.**

CAMPUS LIFE

Help your child notice the admirable traits and talents of friends and others that they might want to acquire.

Promote involvement in campus life which will create a feeling of being connected to others.

BE SELECTIVE

Discuss the effects of excessive drinking, drugs, and partying. Emphasize the need to be responsible even when their college friends are conducting themselves stupidly.

Advise your child to surround themselves with positive, successful people—build friendships. It's OK to tell them that the "nerds" are usually the ones who become very successful.

> Tell them to keep their hopes and dreams alive but to be open to *new ideas*!

KEEPING A GOOD RELATIONSHIP WITH YOUR CHILD

- Avoid overprotecting. Too much assistance may prevent your child from becoming independent. Give them some independence and freedom.

- Don't plan "surprise visits" to the school. Don't plan any family events, outings, celebrations during the last four weeks of the semester.

- If you should call or text and they are too busy to answer, take this as a good sign!

- It's a good idea to tell your child that "Success in college is totally dependent on your self-discipline."

- Accept that you and your child may not have the same long-term and career goals.

- **EXPECT MELTDOWNS TEARS OUTBURSTS OR SILENCE JUST REMEMBER TO BE PATIENT!**

- Limit the number of times you ask your child what he or she is going to do after college.

TAKE CARE THAT YOU CRITICIZE LESS AND LISTEN MORE

Help your child solve his/her own problems. Your child needs to learn how to rise up on his/her own after a setback or disappointment.

At times you and your child may have opposing views on an issue. To avoid unpleasant or heated exchanges, suggest that you set up a specific time to revisit the issue.

Try to keep advice to a minimum unless it is asked for. If you do need to give advice, try to give it in the form of suggestions.

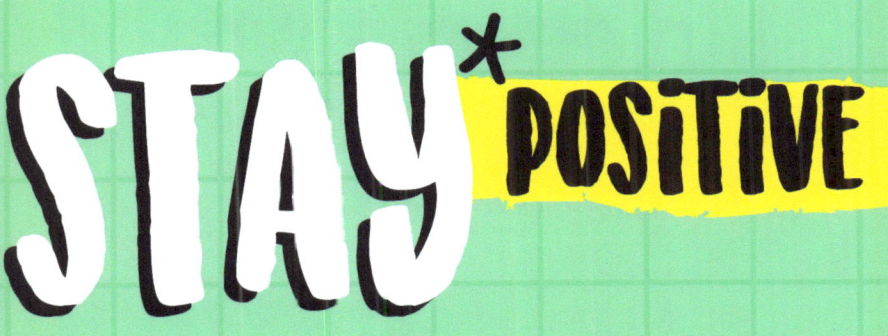

STAY* POSITIVE

It's gratifying to watch your child become an adult. The college years are the time when you start to build an adult relationship.

Accept that you do not have the same control as you did in high school.

I'VE LEARNED THAT PEOPLE WILL FORGET WHAT YOU SAID, PEOPLE WILL FORGET WHAT YOU DID, BUT PEOPLE WILL NEVER FORGET HOW *you made them feel.*

MAYA ANGELOU

Helping ACADEMICALLY

1 FREE TUTORING

Tell them to take advantage of free tutoring even if they are doing well in the class.

Remind them that not all tutoring is remedial; an acceptable essay can benefit from a second pair of eyes.

2 READ BOOKS

Recommend your child read several books from an online college list. Explain how these books will broaden knowledge and strengthen the appreciation of different cultures and times.

3 FREE TIME

Understand that your child will have a lot more free time than when he/she was in high school. About 10% of the time is spent in class and 90% of the time outside of class. Remind them to study well in advance of an exam.

4 LARGE CLASSES

Freshman introductory and lecture classes can be very large (over 200 students). There is very little chance for interaction with the professor, but these classes will often have discussion or study sessions led by a Teaching Assistant (T.A.) or a Graduate Assistant (G.A.). It's possible to get to know the instructor during office hours.

5
SETBACKS

Remember to tell your child that a bad or a failing grade is a setback, and that setbacks and disappointments are a part of life.

6
TELL YOUR CHILD
NO TO PIN ALL THEIR HOPES ON THE FINAL.

7
READING

Understand that one year of high school content is usually packed into one semester of college. Tell your child that the more they read, the better they will become at reading. Good readers are generally well informed.

8
MEETINGS

Tell your child that professors expect students to initiate meetings or to ask for assistance.

9
EDUCATION

Tell your child to go as far as he/she can go with education because education is the one thing that can never be taken away.

10
PROFESSORS

Tell your child that not every professor is a great teacher.

11
EVERYTING PRESENTED
IN CLASS IS FAIR GAME FOR AN EXAM.

12
WORK

Remind your child that unlike high school teachers, professors do not remind students of incomplete work.

Your days of "helping with homework" are over—resist the temptation to edit papers and prepare for tests.

13
THE SYLLABUS

Tell your child that as soon as they receive a syllabus for each class, to read it several times. A syllabus is the contract that has all the rules and assignments. Transfer all important "due dates" to the monthly planner. Make 2 copies of the syllabus—one for their desk and one for their notebook.

14
EDUCATION

Encourage networking. Remind your child to make and maintain connections to the people they will want to keep as friends and those whom they may need in the future.

15
MATH AND SCIENCE

Encourage your child not to shy away from the science and math courses which tend to be difficult and are the courses that lead to higher paying careers. Math and science require precise, diligent instruction in a structured class from a competent instructor. History, sociology, language, political science and other social science and humanities courses are easier to learn and can be learned in a more informal environment such as an online course.

16

Research shows that students who email, text, and listen to music during class remember and understand less and receive lower grades as compared to those who don't.

minds ARE LIKE PARACHUTES

THEY ONLY FUNCTION WHEN OPEN.

LORD THOMAS DEWAR

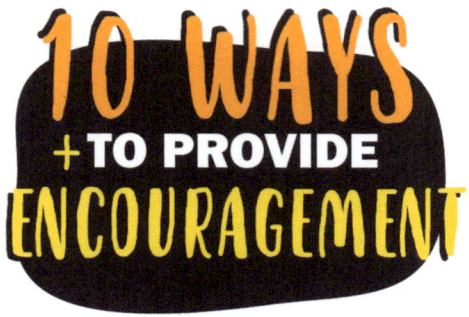

10 WAYS TO PROVIDE ENCOURAGEMENT

+ Encourage your child to study during the day.

+ Encourage your child to keep searching for scholarships by helping in the search. You may even have to take the lead by finding and sending away for application packets.

TELL YOUR CHILD:

- ATTEND COLLEGE CAREER FAIRS
- BECOME A LEADER
- BE OPEN MINDED
- SHOW APPRECIATION FOR DESERVING PEOPLE
- FIGURE OUT SOLUTIONS OR WORK THINGS OUT ON THEIR OWN

+ Tell your child that they do not have to become a "specialist" during the first two years of college. Those are the years to explore and develop a passion to pursue during their lifetime.

+ Encourage your child to do at least 2-3 internships during undergraduate school because internships increase hiring power and many employers place more value on these than a high GPA.

+ Remind your child to associate with quality people.

+ It is normal for everyone to have an occasional "bad day," but if your child reaches out to talk to you about having a string of "bad days" be an attentive listener. Suggest they see a counselor and assure them that doing so is a sign of strength. Also tell them that the student who get counseling have higher graduation rates than those who do not.

> A LONG TIME AGO GILBERT K. WESTERSON SAID:
>
> *THERE IS NO SUCH THING AS AN UNINTERESTING SUBJECT — ONLY UNINTERESTED PEOPLE.*
>
> REMEMBER TO SAY THIS WHEN YOUR CHILD COMPLAINS A CLASS IS BORING.

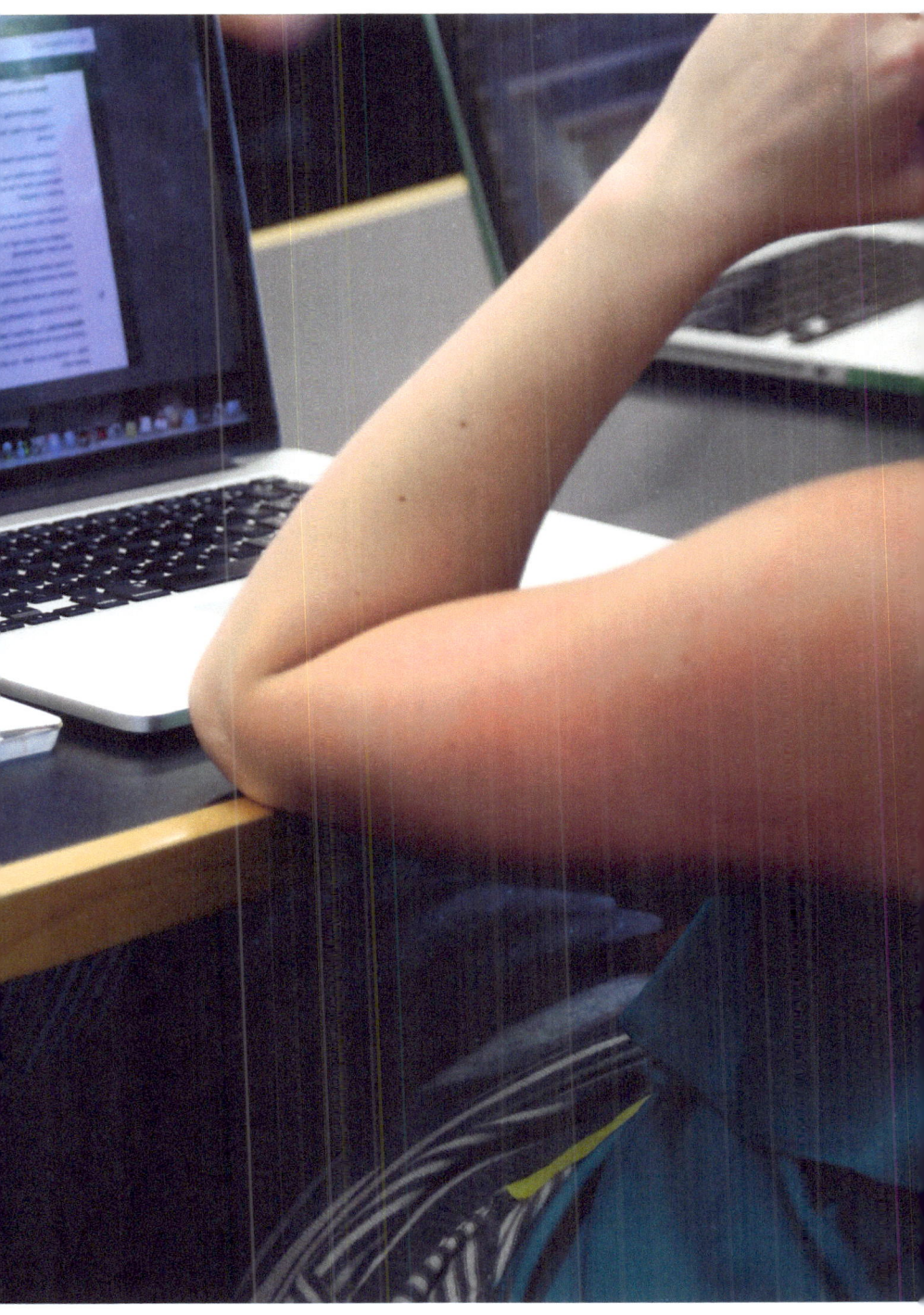

EXTRA CARING gestures

YOU MAY NOT HAVE THOUGHT ABOUT.

1. Teach your child how to be resilient— to bounce back when faced with a difficult situation.

2. Help your child learn how to advocate.

3. If there is a birthday or another special occasion, send a gift card from a local restaurant.

4. Discuss partying, sexual behavior, alcohol and drug use.

5. Tell them that one in three college freshmen don't make it to their sophomore year. Some of the reasons are loneliness, family issues, financial, and academic struggles.

6. Book travel reservations and holiday arrangements at least three months in advance.

7. Teach your child how to calculate tips in restaurants and hair salons.

8. Keep having honest conversations with your child— "How much do you want me to be involved?

9. Surprise them with a greeting card or letter. Send encouraging messages such as *"You sure showed courage," "You have endless talent," "You never cease to make me proud of you."*

10 Discuss the pros and cons of having a part-time job.
Don't pressure your child to come home too often. Discuss what to do if your child should become sick. Find out what the services and care that the health center provides.
Find a local physician in case you need a second opinion.

11 Make sure your child knows how to schedule medical and dental appointments and how to refill prescriptions.

12 Discuss what to do if your child should become sick. Find out what the services and care that the health center provides. Find a local physician in case you need a second opinion.

13 Send a few care packages and ask grandparents, family members, and friends to do the same. Once in a while include an expensive item such as a cosmetic or cologne which they would not be able to buy on their student budget.

14 Discuss how to keep valuables safe. You may want to buy a few extra locks for dorm doors, a bike, jewelry, and luggage. Consider insurance for college.

15 You might want to invest in a foot locker that fits under your child's bed and has a lock. Her private and personal items can be kept there.

16 Know the school's policies toward student drinking and off-campus partying and how they are enforced.

17 The last four weeks of a semester are often the most crucial. This is the time grades might go up or down. Don't plan family get-togethers or campus visits during this time. Give lots of space and explain why.

> *When you teach* **your son** *you teach* **your son's son**
>
> — THE TALMUD

what to EXPECT

EXPECT YOUR CHILD TO HAVE A SHORT TERM CASH EMERGENCY

Expect your child to have a lot of "ups and downs".

Expect Your child's college grades might not be the same as they had in high school.

EXPECT YOUR CHILD TO HAVE CONFLICTS

Expect your child to be homesick and, at times, overemotional and unhappy especially during the first few weeks of college.

Expect your child's interests and preferences to change.

Expect to be puzzled by your children after they have been in college for a semester.

It's OK to let your child know you expect them to graduate in four years by saying:

"We will pay for the first four years of college and after that you're on your own."

Expect your child to call you when things are not going very well. However, most parents report they hear from their child when things are going either very well or when things are very bad.

> "THE PESSIMIST SEES **DIFFICULTY** IN EVERY OPPORTUNITY.
>
> THE OPTIMIST SEES **OPPORTUNITY** IN EVERY DIFFICULTY."
>
> — WINSTON CHURCHILL

PARENTS remember these POINTERS

THE DO'S AND DONT'S
and other tips you should know.

1. Learn how to use Facetime and Skype.

Talk to your child regarding communication. Let your child know when and how much you should be calling or texting.
Set your watch and read for five minutes.

BECOME COMFORTABLE WITH TECHNOLOGY.

2. A big problem most students have is knowing when to ask for help.

*College students will be facing moral and ethical decisions they have never faced before.

INDEPENDENCE IS A GOOD THING!

You will not have the same control but you can still be a big influence.

3. Discuss short and long term goals.

About one-third of college freshmen won't make it back to their sophomore year.

RESIST THE URGE TO MAKE EVERYTHING RIGHT.

4. Having a smart child is great but having a child with a solid work ethic is even greater.

Teach your child to be resilient— how to bounce back with face from a difficult situation.

5. The best skill your child can learn in college is "the ability to learn"

College students usually spend between 12-15 hours a week in class as compared to 30 hours a week in high school. Taking 12 credits a semester is considered full-time but if you want your child to graduate in four years, your child will have to take 15 credits a semester or attend summer sessions.

THE DONT'S

DON'T SAY:
"When I was in college we did it this way."

"Life won't be the same without you."

DON'T ASK:
"Are you homesick?"

Too many questions.

DON'T PLAN:
Many activities over Christmas break because your child has been accustomed to regulating his/her own social life.

Any surprise visits.

DON'T BE:
A helicopter parent.

A helicopter parent sends a subliminal message that they can't handle the situation on their own.

DON'T CRITICIZE:
roommates, friends or professors.

DON'T BE HURT:
if your child discourages you from visiting during the semester.

DON'T DRAG:
out the final goodbye.

DON'T UNDERESTIMATE:
the value of downtime in your child's overscheduled world.

DON'T EXPECT:
the same grades your child earned in high school.

TELL YOUR CHILD
Don't leave your doors unlocked.
Don't walk alone around campus at night. Don't hang around with "losers". Don't ask about grades all the time.

TIP:

YOU LEARN SOMETHING REALLY WELL WHEN YOU USE ALL 4 LEARNING MODES:

VISUAL
AUDITORY
KINESTHETIC
TACTILE

IN OTHER WORDS:
READ ABOUT IT
HEAR ABOUT IT
GIVE IT MOVEMENT
WRITE ABOUT IT

> **BY FAILING TO PREPARE YOU ARE PREPARING TO FAIL.**
>
> — BENJAMIN FRANKLIN

APPENDIX
HANDY COLLEGE TERMS

Academic advisor
Your academic advisor is your on-going "go- to" person who is a consultant, "sounding-board", and the one who has solutions to almost any problem. It is very important that your child establish a relationship since this advisor is assigned for four years. Students are assigned an advisor for their major or catalog year. This advisor helps the student to choose classes.

Academic probation
Students are placed on academic probation if grades fall below a certain level.

Academic suspension
A student placed on suspension usually has one semester to improve grades before dismissal.

"Add" and "Drop"
Students may change their schedule by dropping or adding courses. Each school has a specified time when drops and adds are permitted.

Bursar's Office
This is the office where tuition, fees, fines, and other payments are made.

Co-requisite
A co-requisite is a course which must be taken during the same term as another course.

Dean's List
This is a category for students with high grades. The GPA requirements may vary from school to school.

Early Decision
This is a college administration policy that allows students to commit to attend a school. If a student is accepted early, the student agrees to attend and must withdraw all other applications.

GA
A Graduate Assistant assists in classes by grading papers leading tutoring sessions, and teaching classes.

Helicopter Parent
Helicopter parent made it in the new Merriam Webster Collegiate Dictionary this year. This is a parent who is overinvolved in the life of his/her child. The risk of a helicopter parent is the r children may not become independent.

Internship
An internship is a temporary job, paid or unpaid, usually in the major field. Some internships offer college credit.

Faculty
Teachers in the employ of the college or university. There are several ranks of faculty:

Assistant professor
Entry level tenure tract teaching position at a university.

Associate professor
Once tenure s earned, this is the next level (after assistant professor) of a teaching position.

Tenured professor
The next level teaching position after assistant professor; this usually indicates extensive research and competency in teaching.

Adjunct professor
Professors not on a tenure track (usually part-time)

Blackboard
Blackboard is the online tool that allows faculty to communicate with students such as adding course information and online quizzes.

Mentor
A mentor is someone who teaches, guides, or gives help to a student.

Pass/Fail
Pass/Fail courses earn either a P (Pass) or (F) Fail and not a letter grade.

Pre-requisite
A prerequisite is a class that must be taken before another class. For example, Psychology 101 may be required before Psychology 201.

Provost
The university provost is the chief academic officer who is responsible for the academic curriculum, faculty appointments and university accreditation.

RA
The Resident Assistant or Resident Advisor is a trained leader who supervises those living in a residence hall.

Registrar
The registrar is the official whose responsibility is to maintain current and previous student records.

Resume
A resume is a summary of a person's skills and work experiences often used when applying for a job.

FAFSA
Free Application for Federal Student Aid

GPA
The grade point average is the way most schools rank student academic performance. A = 4 points; B = 3 points; C=2 points; D=1 point; F=0 points.

Audit
Auditing a course allows a student to take a class without receiving a grade or credit. Some students audit courses for the knowledge and/or to prepare for a future course.

Transcript
A transcript is an official document from the college.

College/University
University that shows the completed courses, grades, and dates of attendance.

Stem Courses
The science, technology, engineering, and math courses.

Work-Study
Work-Study are need based; students earn a minimum hourly wage, they are paid hourly for on-campus or off campus jobs. The jobs are usually course related.

Parent Loans
Parents may borrow money to cover costs not covered (PLUS loans) with the student's financial package.

Pell Grants
Pell Grants are need based grants supplied by the government. There is no repayment.

Perkins Loans
Perkin Loans are issued by the school from their allotment of government funds. Nine months after graduation, you begin paying back the loans.

Stafford Loans
Loans offered by banks and credit unions. Stafford Loans are repaid monthly beginning six months after graduation.

Syllabus
Each instructor writes a document that lists the course objectives and requirements. A syllabus is given during the first class meeting.

FERPA
Family Educational Rights and Privacy Act

Withdrawal
Withdrawal is the process of discontinuing a course and a grade of W is recorded on the transcript.

College/University Scolarships
A year before a student intends to go to college, write to the prospective college and university and ask for a list of general scholarships and scholarships specific to the major. If the list is not available, request last year's list.

Support Services
Counseling Centers
Career Centers
Learning Centers
Math Labs
Writing Centers
Wellness Center
Student Gymnasiums and Exercise Center

INDEX

Academic advisor	62
College terms	68-72
Care packages	55
Communicating with child	32, 33, 36, 37, 42, 43
Credit cards	7
Do's and Don'ts	62-64
Encouragement	36, 37, 50, 51
Friends and Peers	40
Expectations	58, 59
Internships	50, 67
Money/Finances/Banking	6, 7
Notification Policy	26
Orientation	18, 20, 21
Parkinson's Law	28
Planner	8, 9, 48
Professor rank	68
Adjunct	69
Assistant	68
Associate	68
Tenure	68
Reading textbooks	68
Sleep/naps	24
Socializing with college friends	22, 36, 40, 41, 48
Support services	72
Student Health Services	20, 55
Campus Police	16
Tutoring Services	46
Syllabus	48, 72
Time	8, 281
Time Wasters	28
Tutoring	46
Warning Signs	32, 33

ACCORDING TO...
(interesting facts and stats)

...the **National Assessment of Educational Progress** (April 27, 2016), commonly referred to as the nation's report card, only 1/3 of 12th graders were ready for college level courses. The percentage of 12th graders who were proficient in reading were:

White	**46%**
Black	**17%**
Hispanic	**25%**
Asian	**49%**
Island Pacific/American Native	**28%**
Two or more races	**45%**
Male	**33%**
Female	**42%**

... **Forbes**, the **15 most valuable college majors for job production growth** and considerable compensation to the year 2020:

Biomedical Engineering
Bio Chemistry
Computer Science
Software Engineering
Environmental Engineering
Civil Engineering
Geology
Information Systems Management
Petroleum Engineering
Applied Mathematics
Mathematics
Construction Management
Finance
Physics
Statistics

THOUGHTS

As a parent, you have "Taken on the Challenge" and succeeded because your child is "off to college." We hope you have enjoyed all of our tips and recommendations and will use many of them.

Remember that your child's college years will be like no other years in both your lives - and they will go very quickly.

We hope your child not only earns the degree but also has a lot of fantastic, enriching experiences. We also hope you keep this book handy and reread it before every semester begins!

Kay Lopate and Patsy Self Trand

P.S. Don't forget to fill out the letter to yourself on the following pages during graduation week!!

You are now the proud parent of a college graduate.

On the next page, write another letter to yourself during the week of your child's graduation. Again, each paragraph begins with a sentence starter. All you need to do is add 2-3 sentences to complete the paragraph. You will be glad you did this and you will treasure these memories years from now.

Again, congratulations to your graduate, and congratulations especially to you.

Graduation date: _____

Dear: _____

As I prepare for my child to walk across the stage I feel:
_____
_____ about graduation.

I also feel: _____

I'm a little nervous about: _____

All in all, the college experience has been: ___
_____
_____

To celebrate graduation, we plan to: _____
_____
_____

I have invited the following people to attend the graduation ceremony: _____
_____
_____

After graduation, my child plans to: _____
All in all, I think my child's college experience has been: _____
and the reasons are: _____

Regards to myself,

About the AUTHORS

Kay Lopate is a Professor Emeritus from the University of Miami, Miami, FL where she co-founded the Reading and Study Skills Center and taught for College of Education. Her special interests are preparing PreMed students for medical school and helping undergraduate students acquire advanced reading abilities to succeed in the demands of mastering college level textbooks.

Patsy Self Trand is a faculty member of Florida International University and former administrator of the Reading and Learning Lab. Dr. Trand teaches undergraduate, honors, and graduate courses for the FIU School of Arts and Sciences. She is committed to pass her wealth of knowledge and experience to help high school and college students reach their academic goals. She has authored many articles and has presented at many national and international conferences.

www.ingramcontent.com/pod-product-compliance
Lightning Source LLC
Chambersburg PA
CBHW042331150426
43194CB00001B/19